W9-CCG-987

Celebrate the Seasons!

It's Spring!

By Linda Glaser

Illustrated by Susan Swan

The Millbrook Press   Brookfield, Connecticut

To Suzanne, a passionate nature lover and dear friend, who has shared many natural wonders with me—both large and small.
LG

For Celeste Rasberry, who is a joy in any season!
SS

Library of Congress Cataloging-in-Publication Data
Glaser, Linda.
It's spring! / by Linda Glaser; illustrated by Susan Swan.
p. cm. — (Celebrate the seasons!)
Summary: A child observes the arrival of spring and its effects on plants and animals.
Includes suggestions for nature study projects.
ISBN 0-7613-1760-0 (lib. bdg.) 0-7613-1345-1 (pbk.)
[1. Spring—Fiction. 2. Nature—Fiction.] I. Swan, Susan, ill. II. Title. III. Series.
PZ7.G48047 lu 2002 [E]—dc21 2001018709

Published by:
The Millbrook Press, Inc.
2 Old New Milford Road
Brookfield, Connecticut 06804
www.millbrookpress.com

Printed in Hong Kong
lib: 5 4 3 2 1
tr: 5 4 3 2 1

It's
Spring!

I run outside in thin pants and short sleeves.
No thick heavy winter coat bundled around me.
I skip and leap and feel light and free.
Fresh air rushes all over me.

Creeks and streams are starting to flow.
We hear the trickle of melting ice and snow.
Then one day, pitter patter, splitter splatter.
Rain pours down. Creeks and streams rush
and gush again.

I dip my boot in a puddle just to see how deep it is.
Swish swish. Watch this.
KER-SPLASH! It's spring!

We find tight pointy leaf buds on bushes and trees. I peel one open and see the tiny beginnings of fresh new leaves. I find some pussy willows. They look soft and sleek. I rub one gently against my cheek.

The ground is growing soft and warm again.
There's a clean fresh smell in the air.
We find tiny new green growing things everywhere.

Animals that slept all winter are now waking up—
earthworms, frogs, turtles, snakes, beetles, ladybugs.

One day we spot a robin.
Then soon we see red-winged blackbirds and
a bright goldfinch. Early in the morning we
hear the birds sing. They cheep and warble
and trill—it's spring!

Birds fly here and there with grass in their beaks. We watch them building nests in trees—getting ready for new families. Squirrels line their nests with sticks and dry leaves. And here in this hole are new baby bunnies.

Ducks quack to their ducklings, and geese honk to their goslings—all soft and fuzzy and out for a swim.

Day by day I watch flower buds grow and swell.
Soon they burst open into bright daffodils—
so sunny and cheerful they make my heart sing.
It's spring!

Ferns uncurl. Leaves unfurl. Tree branches that were bare now have tiny green leaves. It's time to plant seeds! Corn, cucumbers, beans, peas, and my very own sunflower seeds.

The days are getting longer. Now the sun sets *after* dinner. Outside, we watch the sky turn slowly dark and count the stars as they come out. Then all the spring peepers and bullfrogs sing. It's spring!

The sun shines longer, and the days grow warmer.
One day I notice that the trees are all covered
with full-grown leaves. Soon it will be summer.
But right now, it's still spring.

I blow dandelion seed fluff and watch it float away.
Dragonflies dip and dart every which way.

I leap in the air. There's new life bursting everywhere.
Come out! Smell the flowers! Hear the birds sing!
It's spring!

Nature Activities to Do in the Spring

Watch birds flying with dry grasses in their beaks. See if you can spot one building a nest.

Take the hair out of your hairbrush and put it outside for a bird to use to line its nest.

If you find a nest where baby birds have hatched, watch how the parents care for them. But stay far enough away so you don't frighten or disturb them.

Put up a bird feeder. Feed the birds. They can use the extra help in spring because very little food is left after winter. And there's not much ready to eat yet.

Listen to birds singing. Try to identify some birds by their calls.

See if you can find pictures of animals like snowshoe hares, ptarmigan, and ermines with "changing" coloring. Spring is the time their fur or feathers change from winter white to summer brown.

Collect some earthworms. Put them in a large jar with moist (not wet) dirt. Wrap black construction paper around the jar. Each day, unwrap the black paper and watch the earthworms tunneling. After a few days, put the earthworms back outside.

Visit a stream with a
grown-up and notice
the ice melting. As the
days grow warmer, you may see
tadpoles. Collect a few in a jar
filled with stream water. Watch
them for the day. Then return them to the stream.

At night go to a pond or stream with a grown-up and listen to the frogs
singing.

Plant a small tree this spring. Watch it grow year after year. Each year
in the spring, take a picture of yourself next to the tree. Watch how both
of you grow each year.

On May Day (May 1) fill a basket with flowers and a treat to eat.
Ring a friend's doorbell and leave the May basket sitting there as a
special surprise.

Examine leaf buds closely through a magnifying glass. Carefully open
one. See if you can find the tiny beginnings of leaves.

Clip some pussy willow stalks. Put them in a vase without water. That
way they will stay just as they are. If you put them in a vase with water,
you can watch them grow and change.

Pick some spring flowers. Arrange them in a vase filled with water. Make sure to ask a grown-up which flowers you may pick.

With a grown-up, find a pond where there are ducklings, goslings, or cygnets (baby swans). Visit regularly to watch them grow.

Plant beans in a pot on the windowsill. Water them and watch them grow.

Help plant your own garden—either in a big pot or in the yard. Some fast-growing and good-tasting vegetables for a child's garden are leaf lettuce, baby carrots, bush beans, and green peas. Some fun vegetables that take longer but are favorites of many children are cherry tomatoes, gourds, cucumbers, and pumpkins.

Plant a flower garden. Many flowers can be bought as small plants. Some easy flowers that you can grow from seed and that bloom in one growing season are bachelor's buttons, cosmos, marigolds, nasturtiums, and sunflowers. Remember to water them!

About the Author and Illustrator

Linda Glaser is the author of many successful nonfiction picture books on natural history subjects. Her books SPECTACULAR SPIDERS, COMPOST!, WONDERFUL WORMS, and OUR BIG HOME: AN EARTH POEM were all named Outstanding Science Trade Books for Children by the Children's Book Council/National Science Teachers Association. In addition to teaching and writing, she conducts writing workshops for schoolchildren and for adults. She lives in Minnesota.

For IT'S SPRING!, Susan Swan created three-dimensional cut-paper artwork. First she selected her papers and then hand painted them to get the colors and textures she needed to achieve the palette of spring. She then cut and layered the papers to accomplish the dramatic sense of depth that gives life to each piece of art. Finally, Susan's husband, Terry, photographed the finished artwork with lighting that accents the shadows of the paper. Susan and her husband are, professionally, Swan & Rasberry Studios, and they live in Texas.